Half Round the World

CHRISTINE HARRIS
Illustrated by Rachel Tonkin

KINGSCOURT/McGRAW-HILL

Halfway Round the World
Copyright © 2001 Rigby Heinemann

Rigby is part of Harcourt Education, a division of
Reed International Books Australia Pty Ltd ABN 70 001 002 357.

Text by Christine Harris
Illustrations by Rachel Tonkin
Designed by Andrew Cunningham

Published in the United Kingdom by Kingscourt/McGraw-Hill,
a division of the MH Companies. All rights reserved. No part of this
publication may be reproduced or distributed in any form or by any
means, or stored in a database or retrieval system, without the prior
written consent of Kingscourt/McGraw-Hill, including, but not limited
to, network or other electronic storage or transmission, or broadcast
for distance learning. Originally published in Australia by Rigby
Heinemann, a division of Reed International Books Australia Pty Ltd.

KINGSCOURT/McGRAW-HILL

Shoppenhangers Road, Maidenhead
Berkshire, SL6 2QL
Telephone: 01628 502730
Fax: 01628 635895

www.kingscourt.co.uk
E-mail: enquiries@kingscourt.co.uk

Printed in Australia by Advance Press

10 9 8 7 6 5 4 3 2 1

ISBN: 0-07-710328-9

Contents

Chapter 1 The Hope 1

Chapter 2 Below Decks 14

Chapter 3 Pirate Scare 38

Chapter 4 Alice Constance Collins 53

Chapter 5 A Rescue 63

Chapter 6 A Promise Kept 73

Chapter One

The Hope

MATTHEW EDGED forward in the queue, his heart thumping. He shifted his bag from one hand to the other, then wiped his sweaty palm down the leg of his trousers. He must not appear nervous.

He had passed the medical test. All the doctor had done was ask if he felt sick, then told him to poke out his tongue. Now he had to get on board. Soon, the sailor at the gangway of the *Hope* would finish checking the family with children who wriggled like worms. Then it would be Matthew's turn. That would be the point of danger.

Would his life now go forward or backwards? Forward to a new land of sunshine and freedom, or back again to mucking out stables. He had sworn to his dying father that he would board the *Hope*. It was the most important promise of his life and he was determined to keep it.

Finally, the children in front of Matthew were pushed, pulled and cajoled over the gangplank and onto the decks of the ship by their parents. The mother, a solid woman with puffy cheeks, spoke snappily to the girl beside her. "Caroline, that blush is unbecoming. You are drawing attention to yourself. Stop it immediately."

The girl's face went even redder. She turned aside and grabbed the hand of a toddler who was crying and calling out, "I'm hungry."

"Name?" The sailor held a wad of papers in his hands. He snapped out his question without looking up.

Matthew took a deep breath before attempting to reply. At that same moment, a rooster crowed loudly. Matthew's words were cut off just as he began them.

The sailor looked up from his list and raised one eyebrow.

"Er, m...my name is M...Matthew Francis." He felt his face flame. His careful concentration had failed. His first words at the *Hope's* gangplank were stuttered. It happened more often when he was nervous. And today, nervous didn't begin to describe how he felt.

With a grubby finger, the sailor traced down the rows of letters. A sting of envy shot through Matthew. If he could read, he could see for himself if his name was on the list.

"Aye. Here it is," said the sailor. "And Jack Francis?"

"M...my father."

"Just as well. The captain doesn't hold with children travelling on their own on his ship. Too much trouble. But a man's got to make a living." The sailor leaned towards Matthew and whispered, "There's some that say the captain was never a boy himself, that he suddenly appeared one day as a whole man." There was an odd glint from beneath the sailor's bushy eyebrows.

Matthew turned, spied a plump gentleman in the queue behind him, and waved. He gave the widest grin his mouth would allow. There was the shortest of pauses before the man waved back. With any luck, the sailor would assume that man was his father and they had simply become separated in the crush of passengers.

"Oi, Harry!" A second sailor pushed through the crowd on deck. With his hands cupped around his mouth, he shouted, "Captain says hurry it up. The wind's freshening and he wants to catch the tide."

Matthew held his breath.

The sailor called Harry nodded toward the *Hope*. "Look sharp, lad. If the captain says jump, you ask, 'How high?' Soon as we set sail, you watch him call for a bucket of seawater to wash his face in. 'Washing off the land' he calls it. Next!"

Head down, Matthew scuttled across the gangplank. Now he had to find his way below decks and stay out of sight till they were clear of land. Then it would be too late to put him off the ship. Besides, he didn't want to watch the country of his birth shrink into the distance and disappear. It was difficult enough as it was. He was alone, and about to sail halfway round the world, into the unknown.

Easing his way around passengers, crates and coiled ropes, Matthew headed towards a hatchway. Another sailor was trying to organise the passengers into various parts of the ship. A puckered scar across his forehead made his right eye appear lower than the left. What had split his head like that? He looked up. "Steerage?" he asked.

Matthew nodded uneasily.

"Down." The sailor pointed.

Matthew peered down the hatchway. The ladder looked dangerous, the lower level of the ship dark and unwelcoming. Free passage meant he had no choice about where they put him. The sailor grabbed Matthew's bag. "Be quick. The tide's turning and the captain doesn't like to be kept waiting." Leaning over, he shouted, "Look out below." Then he dropped the bag through the hatchway.

A yelp echoed up from the lower depths of the ship. The sailor with the crooked eyes just shrugged and scurried away. Immediately, a head appeared at the top of the open hatchway. A broad-shouldered young man roared at him, "Was that your bag, runt?"

Runt, the smallest of the litter, weakling. It was not the first time someone had applied that name to his skinny frame. Matthew tried to explain, but the words became tangled. "I...I...it..."

The young man on the ladder laughed, but it wasn't the sound of someone sharing a joke. "What's that on your boots?"

Matthew looked down. Evidence that he had been in a horse stable was squashed on his shabby boots.

The young man pinched his nostrils together with one hand. "Phew. Maybe you'd better bunk on deck with the animals. You'd fit right in."

Matthew froze, not knowing what to say.

"Listen. I'm warning you. Stay out of my way," ordered the young man.

That would probably be impossible. There was a four month journey ahead.

Matthew felt his spirits sink even lower. They hadn't even set sail yet and already he had made an enemy.

Matthew leaned against the bulwark and stared at the water curling away from the bow. There was nothing but the ship, the sea and the sky. No sign of land and safety.

The sailors chanted as they hauled on ropes to rearrange the order of the sails. Matthew had never seen so many ropes, hanging from the sails and coiled in neat piles on the decks. How did they know what rope was for which sail?

Some of the passengers downstairs had issued warnings to each other. "Don't go up on deck. Fresh air's bad for you. You'll get sick." Matthew shook his head. For years, he and his father had worked outdoors and they had been no sicker than anyone else, probably less. "People are foolish when they're afraid," his father had sometimes told him. "Don't mind them too much."

But he did mind. He couldn't help it. And he minded that his father was not here to give him that advice again, even if he had heard it a hundred times. His father had a slip of advice for every occasion. Matthew thought of him as a book without the writing. Only now that book was closed.

In the hours since they had left shore, Matthew had hidden among the crowd in the dimness below deck. Every minute, he had expected a hand to grab his collar and haul him up to the captain.

"Does a man good to fill his lungs with salty air," said a voice beside him.

Matthew started. A man with hollow cheeks, a hooked nose and hair that was a little too long, stood beside him. Not knowing what to say, Matthew simply nodded, then turned back to the water heaving out from the bow. He was not one for small talk. He could never think of any.

Suddenly, the man grabbed his wrist. "I wouldn't be doing that if I was you." He threw a glance at the crew members who were still hauling on ropes. "Sailors are a superstitious lot."

"W...what?"

The man let go of his wrist with an apologetic grin. "Whistling."

It was such a habit, Matthew had not realised he was doing it.

"You're a fine whistler, lad, but it's bad luck at sea. There's some that believe you whistle up the wind."

A quick glance at the man's face showed only kind concern.

"D...do you think that's true?"

The man shrugged. "People believe what they have a mind to believe. But I've sailed with a man they said could whistle up the wind. When we hit the doldrums, there wasn't any wind at all for weeks.

We were running out of food. So the captain ordered this man to whistle up the wind again. He refused, said he couldn't do it. Captain had him clapped in irons until he obeyed. That night, the man whistled and a strong wind sprang up."

"The wind might have happened anyway, whether the man whistled or not."

"Aye." The man's voice held a note of doubt, as though he was not convinced. "Seeing as we're going to be shipmates for the next few months, I'm thinking we should be introducing ourselves properly." He held out his left hand. "Timothy Maslin, retired seaman."

Awkwardly, Matthew shook Timothy's hand. "I...I'm Matthew Francis."

"Pleased to meet you, that I am, Matthew Francis."

Matthew looked away. The wind whipped their faces to a healthy red as they watched waves dance drunkenly across the surface of the ocean.

"W...why does the ship zigzag?" asked Matthew. "W...wouldn't it be quicker to sail in a straight line?"

Timothy turned his body to face him. An empty sleeve cuff flopped against his right side. There was nothing but space where his hand should have been. Matthew quickly looked away. He did not want Timothy to catch him staring. It might hurt his feelings.

"It's the back sails, you see," answered Timothy. "If we sailed straight, they'd stop the wind reaching the other sails. But if the ship tacks left and right and the wind is side-on, then all the sails catch the wind." He sniffed. "Sea air whets a man's appetite. I hear cook's aiming to have strike-me-blind for supper."

At Matthew's confused expression, Timothy laughed. "Boiled rice."

For the first time in days, Matthew felt an impulse to laugh back. But, abruptly, the laughter died in his throat.

"Can you smell something?" asked a voice that he recognised.

A prickling sensation began at the back of Matthew's neck. It was the young man who had shouted at him earlier. His name was Roger.

"Maybe," replied a second voice. "Could be seaweed, Roger."

Roger's voice was loud. Instinctively, Matthew knew Roger wanted him to hear his words. Matthew stared out at the ocean, resisting the temptation to check his boots. He had scraped them clean.

"Cook reckons the captain doesn't have the bones of a man, like us," said Roger. "He has whale bones under his skin. And he keeps a cat-o'-ninetails beside him whenever he's on the quarterdeck. If anyone even looks at him the wrong way, he thrashes them."

Matthew felt Timothy's curious gaze, but he didn't return it. He stood as rigidly as a stone statue.

"The captain isn't too pleased either," said Roger. "They reckon there's someone missing. Some fellow called Jack."

Chapter Two

Below Decks

MATTHEW FUMBLED with the ropes on his hammock. He wished he had a wooden bunk like the married couples. But at least he had the hammock to himself. Some of the bunks were assigned to whole families. How would any of them sleep squashed like fish in a basket?

This knot would never do. As soon as his weight landed on the canvas, the ropes would slip and he would crash onto the floor. He paused for a second, trying not to breathe in too deeply. The inside of the ship smelt strongly of musty, damp wood.

For the first time in his life, he was glad he was short. The ceiling was so low, already several cries told of collisions between heads and wood. And as they sailed further from shore, the more the wind whipped the waves. It made his stomach flutter.

He sneaked a look over at the far wall. Roger was seated with his back propped against the wall, swapping stories with his companion. He had said nothing to Matthew, nor even looked at him. Perhaps it was only coincidence that he had talked about a missing passenger up on deck.

Timothy appeared, smiling down his hooked nose as though he was amused.

"If you were wanting to tie those knots yourself, that's fine with me. I'm not a man to interfere. But I can show you a really grand knot that would hold the weight of two cows."

The idea of two cows snoozing in a hammock made Matthew smile. With his right fingers and with a little steadying from the stump of his left arm, Timothy knotted the rope. "Ropes and I are well acquainted. A rope stole my arm."

Matthew's gaze was drawn back to Timothy's damaged arm, with its lower quarter missing.

"I was up the mast of a ship in a storm when it snapped in two. I hope I never see the likes of it again. The sea was like a living monster. If it couldn't swallow us right away, it would smash us to pieces."

Matthew shuddered. He could almost hear the creak of stressed timber, the heavy roar of waves, the wind whistling through the ropes and hurling itself with loud booms onto the canvas sails. As if in

response, the *Hope* lurched to one side. There was a surge of voices from the other steerage passengers. Perhaps they, too, had not previously been to sea.

"My hand was tangled in the ropes. The mast was dragging in the sea, with me attached to it…"

I wouldn't have to drown, thought Matthew, I would have died of fright. Then he wondered why it was that in his mind, his voice was firm and strong and he never stuttered. Not once. Something happened when the words reached his lips.

"It was either say goodbye to my life or my hand. I chose to part with my hand." Timothy chuckled. "After all, I did have another one."

How could this man go through something so terrible and laugh about it?

It didn't take Timothy long to have the hammock firmly secured. The ship lurched again and Matthew staggered. Timothy appeared not to notice.

"Hey!"

They both turned to look in the direction the voice was coming from.

"I'd already spoken for that place for my hammock," said Roger, then inclined his head towards the young man next to him. "Tell them it's true."

"It's true." His friend repeated the words like a trained parrot.

"You should have checked first." Roger's tone was determined.

Matthew knew there was no difference between these pegs in the wall and the next set. Roger had waited until the hammock was firmly secured before complaining. Matthew felt Timothy's green eyes staring at him, expecting him to say something.

Pride urged Matthew to refuse to move, but common sense told him that Roger was a lot bigger than he was. One hard punch and Matthew's teeth would sit at the back of his head instead of the front. Besides, there were many weeks to endure in close contact with Roger. Best not to antagonise him more than he already had.

"S...s...sorry."

Roger snorted.

Hot stinging began at the back of Matthew's eyes.

Without a word, Timothy moved the hammock to the further end of their designated area.

Then two feet appeared at the top of the wooden ladder. As the owner descended, Matthew saw a pair of legs in loose trousers, then a checked shirt. It was the sailor called Harry. "Matthew Francis?"

Matthew put up his hand.

"On deck. Now. Captain wants you."

Captain Baldwin stood, feet apart, hands clasped behind his back. Only officers were allowed on the quarterdeck. Matthew had to wait at the bottom of the short stairway.

He did not speak or look at Matthew. And Matthew did not want to irritate him by speaking out of turn. Captain Baldwin gave an order to the man beside him, who repeated it at the top of his voice, both hands cupped around his mouth. The wind ruffled Matthew's hair and made his eyes run. In the last hour, the wind had increased. The sea was becoming rougher.

Matthew could not see a cat-o'-ninetails anywhere. Once, he had seen a squire punish his servant with one of those. The cat-o'-ninetails had sliced the servant's back. Was the captain allowed to thrash passengers? Even if he wasn't, who could stop him? Matthew's stomach turned a somersault.

Passengers were peering over the bulwark, staring at the sea. But there were fewer of them now. Most had gone below deck as the weather freshened. And those who braved the stinging wind, huddled together, jackets tightly clasped. The bucking motion of the ship made Matthew's stomach swirl like the ocean.

Finally, the captain looked down at

Matthew. His eyes were the colour of the sea on a fine day, with deep-set wrinkles clustered around them. Matthew stood to attention, his back as straight as a perfect length of timber.

"Your name?" asked Captain Baldwin.

"M...Matthew F...Francis, sir."

Captain Baldwin's sea-blue eyes seemed to bore right into Matthew's head. He felt exposed, and dreadfully alone.

"How old are you, boy?"

Hesitantly, Matthew told him, then added, "I...I've b...been earning my own w...way for two years now, s...sir."

"Hard work never hurt anyone."

Matthew nodded.

"There are several things you should know about me..." The captain broke off to shout at the sailor with the puckered brow. He had obviously done something wrong. The sailor hung his head and then scuttled off.

"I don't like insolence, laziness or loose ends, boy. Understand me? Life is untidy enough as it is." His blue eyes fired. "Are you a loose end?"

Matthew shook his head.

"Where's Jack Francis, your relative?"

"Uh..." Matthew took a deep breath and concentrated on pronouncing each syllable carefully so he wouldn't stutter too much. "He's...he couldn't come, sir. B...but he made me promise that I'd sail anyw...way."

"Why couldn't he come?" The captain's voice was still controlled, but louder.

A wave splashed over the lower deck and a woman squealed. The ship leaned to one side, the sails straining.

"H...he died." Matthew hadn't wanted to say the word, not out loud. It made it so final. There was no pretending that his father would ever again be scrubbing his face and hands in the old tub after work. Nor would he ever be whispering to a mare in foal or ruffling Matthew's hair when he was enthusiastic.

"Unattended children are not permitted on board my ship."

"My passage to Australia has been paid for, by the government."

"Just as well," snapped the captain, or

you'd spend the trip working till the skin peeled off your hands." He sniffed. "Or in irons. Don't hold with thieves. Been to countries where they cut off your hands if you take something that's not yours."

Matthew thought of Timothy's empty sleeve. And, as if his thought had summoned up the real person, Timothy appeared beside him. "Begging your pardon, Captain."

Two blue eyes swivelled to the lower deck in Timothy's direction. The captain frowned. "Do I know you?"

"Yes, sir. Timothy Maslin. We sailed on the *Julianna* together. I was just a cabin boy back then, and you were first mate."

Recognition passed over the captain's features, the hard lines on his face softened. "It was a wild ship that one."

"Aye, Captain. And you were the only one who could tame her."

The captain made a noise of dismissal, but his eyes showed he was pleased by the compliment.

"You were always fair, Captain. Tough, as you should be. But fair as needed."

"Is this leading somewhere?"

"The boy's been a big help to me." Timothy raised his arm and showed the loose cuff where a wrist should be.

"Are you willing to be responsible for the boy, Mr Maslin?"

"Aye, Captain. It would be a big favour to me. He's a good lad."

Captain Baldwin turned his gaze back to the horizon. "Don't bring yourself to my attention again, Matthew Francis."

Matthew opened his mouth to speak, then felt his stomach lurch more drunkenly than the ship. He dashed to the bulwark, hung his head over the side and, violently, loudly, began heaving his stomach out.

"Am I g...going to die?" Matthew groaned as his hammock swung with the movement of the ship.

"No, lad. You're young and healthy. You're just seasick. It'll pass. I've seen it many a time, and worse."

Matthew could not see Timothy's face in the darkness, but it was reassuring to hear him speak.

"What's that smell?" he asked.

"Stagnant bilge water stirred up by the storm. It's enough to melt the hair up a man's nostrils," said Timothy.

To distract himself from the sounds of other passengers' seasickness and from the thick, humid air below decks, Matthew tried to think of pleasant things about home. He remembered the first blossoms of spring, the warm steam that rose from a newborn foal, the clip-clop of horses' hooves on cobblestone and the sweet scent of fresh hay.

Thoughts of home only made Matthew feel worse. He could not think of it without picturing his father and his loss was too raw, too new. He felt himself gagging and reached for the bucket that Timothy had tucked beside him in the hammock. How could he be sick again? Already, he felt as though he had turned himself inside out. He swallowed and forced himself to lie calmly, not giving in to his sudden urge.

Waves crashed against the ship with a mighty thump, as though powerful arms had swung a sledgehammer. Surrounded by darkness, hatches secured to stop the sea from pouring in, Matthew was terrified the ship would sink and they would all be trapped below decks.

A flicker of light from the families' bunks advertised that someone had ignored the rules and lit an oil lamp. "No smoking below decks, no lamps after 10 p.m. and no cooking unless supervised in the galley by the cook," they had been told. But this time, fear of the dark in the storm was stronger than fear of the captain's wrath.

At least there was one good side to all of

Below Decks   27

this. Roger was too ill to bother anyone. His loud moans testified to that.

"They have animals in Australia that jump on their back legs. They're the size of a human," said Timothy. "They carry their young in pouches on their stomachs. I've seen many things, but not that."

Matthew knew Timothy was chatting to distract him from his misery, and he was grateful.

"They say the sun always shines and there are birds that laugh at you."

How could the sun always be shining?

They would need rain for drinking water. Still, the idea was a cheerful one.

"W...what's the most amazing thing y...you've ever seen?" Matthew turned his head to look at Timothy. The lamp light flickered and it was dull, but now he could see Timothy's outline. His good hand was tucked behind his head as he swung in his hammock, with no sign of queasiness.

"Well, now. Let me think. There was the fisherman in the Fiji islands who fell overboard. His friends thought it was too dangerous to pick him up so they sailed on without him. A few days later he staggered ashore on his island, exhausted but alive. He'd found his way home by feeling the wind on his ears and knowing from which direction the winds came."

Timothy cleared his throat. "But the most amazing thing...was the expression in my Mary's eyes when she smiled at me. Two years it was before my ship returned. She had thought I was never coming back. By then, she belonged to someone else. But I saw it, that look. It's not something a man would be forgetting."

Matthew struggled to think of something comforting to say. He knew how it felt to lose someone you cared about.

"Argh. I wouldn't be wishing the life of a sailor's wife on anyone," said Timothy. "And who'd be wanting a man with only one hand?"

"I d...don't notice. Really," said Matthew. "N...not after the first glance."

"That's mighty nice of you, lad. Although there's some that only see what's missing and not what's there."

"W...well, you can feel sorry for them. For all those things they don't see." Matthew remembered Timothy's deft knot-tying. "Anyway, you can do more things with one hand than most people can do with two."

"That's a fine way of looking at the situation."

The *Hope* bucked left and right like a frightened animal.

A cry came from nearby. "There's water coming in."

One quick glance over the side of the hammock and Matthew saw it was true.

Water covered the floor to the depth of a man's ankle. A shoe floated past, then a scrap of material.

"We're all going to drown!"

Timothy's voice was reassuring. "Don't you fret, lad. It's only the fear of someone who doesn't know the sea. It could get worse than this and we'd stay afloat. The crew will be manning the pumps, lad. I trust the captain. He's the best sailor I ever saw."

"Is it t...true there are no lifeboats for the steerage passengers?"

"Aye." Timothy's tone showed he did not like it either. "But you're safer on the ship than in small lifeboats on this sea. They call waves like this 'grey widow-makers'. No, we're much better off right where we are."

Matthew's hammock swung out from one side to the other. His stomach heaved with the movement.

"And you've got a hammock," added Timothy. "When you roll it up each morning, trick is to do it as tight as you can, then wind the rope around it. If it was needed, it'd keep you afloat for a while."

Every timber in the ship seemed to groan with the strain of staying upright. Matthew could scarcely swallow over the nervous lump that formed in his throat.

"There's a good rule I learnt on my first journey," said Timothy, "You only worry when the captain looks nervous."

True, Captain Baldwin had not looked nervous earlier on as the sea was roughing up. However, the storm had worsened. What would Captain Baldwin's face show now, with the sea rising like a mountain?

"What about you, Matthew lad. What are you wanting to see in this grand new land we're going to?"

Matthew tried to picture the future but it was blank. What had previously seemed like an adventure, now seemed only a duty without his father. He felt an awful dread that they would never reach this wondrous land. The ship would sink and no-one would know for months that their bodies lay trapped at the bottom of the ocean. Matthew shivered as his spirits sank like the imagined ship.

"A man can't spend his whole life looking backwards. He'd trip over everything in his path," said Timothy. "Always remember what's behind, but look forward to what's ahead. There must be something you want to do or see."

Matthew remembered Timothy's comment about the sun always shining.

"A b…blue sky. B…blue all the way across from one side to the other."

"Aye. Now that would be grand."

The thud of water against wood came as the *Hope* slewed to one side. Screams erupted. The ship righted, then lurched in the opposite direction. Personal items not secured, cracked and smashed onto the wooden floorboards. A child rolled out of its bunk and onto the floor with a splash and was hauled back by his father.

Matthew felt his stomach contract. Another wild careering of the ship smashed the lamp.

"Fire!" Someone screamed. "We have to get out. The ship's on fire!"

Matthew clenched his fingers into tight fists. The darkness was overwhelming.

Shouts, screams, wild splashing and thumps came from all around him as the passengers panicked. They were trying to get to the ladder and above decks, all at the same time.

He struggled to sit, so he could swing his legs over the side of his hammock. Being caught down here in a fire would be worse than drowning. He was aware of Timothy's voice, but his words were smothered by the terrific noise of a human stampede.

Trembling with weakness, Matthew hoisted his body over the side of his hammock, half-falling into the water that slopped across the floor. He felt a moment of terror as the cold seawater splashed up his legs. For a second, he stood without moving, waiting for the water to suck his legs down into its icy depths.

"D...don't be stupid," he shouted at his fears. The water was only a few inches deep. He turned in the direction of the ladder and freedom. His legs felt like jelly, not strong enough to support his body.

"Open the hatch. Open the hatch!" Above the rabble, came the repeated chant of many voices calling for attention. People were trying to force their way out.

Someone ran full pelt into him, knocking him off his feet. Barely a second later, a heavy weight landed on his fingers. He yelped and snatched back his hand. A loud splash suggested whoever had trodden on his hand had overbalanced and fallen flat in the water. If only he could see what was happening. Why didn't they lift the hatch?

A thought was trying to break through the panic in his mind, trying to speak to him. But the noisy confusion and the pain in his hand stopped him from listening.

"T...Timothy!" Matthew shouted, trying to stand up. It was useless. Timothy would never hear him above the ruckus.

Halfway to his feet, an object again barrelled into Matthew, knocking him backwards. Automatically, his arms closed around the object, a small body. He sat, totally saturated now, his canvas hammock dragging on his head. He must be underneath it. Awkwardly, he struggled to sit.

Two arms squeezed his neck. Small arms. They belonged to a child.

The child made no sound, but Matthew could feel it trembling like a leaf in a strong wind. Instinctively, he slid his own arms around the small body and held it close. A child this size could be trampled before the flames or water could get close. He must not let go, whatever happened.

Matthew clambered to his feet. He had to get to the ladder and upstairs, taking the child with him. It clung to him tightly, like a snail to its shell. He could sense the child's terror, an echo of his own.

"Don't be s...scared," he said. "I'll g...get you out of here."

The child gripped harder. If it was any stronger, it might choke him.

Then, clearly, coldly, a thought pierced his consciousness. It was pitch black still. No light, no flickering flames, no smoke—there was no fire.

A week later, Matthew still had trouble sleeping. Each time the last lamp was extinguished and the lower deck subsided into darkness, he could not help a moment of panic, reliving the riot.

No crew member had opened the hatch that night. He had tried to tell himself that because of the storm's fury, no-one above decks had heard them. But he could not really believe it. When he had asked Timothy about it, Timothy had mumbled a vague reply about not filling up the holds with water. But there was something else in his eyes, something unspoken. If the fire had been real and not just a false alarm, Matthew dreaded to think what would have happened.

Chapter Three

Pirate Scare

MATTHEW SHOOK his head to clear the disturbing memory and slid a peg onto his wet shirt. The stormy seas had subsided to a clear, calm surface. The sun smiled through patches of white cloud, so all the bedding was spread over the deck, airing. Washed clothes hung over the sail rigging and any other available place to dry.

A tug at Matthew's trouser leg made him look down. Alice, the little girl who had clung to him on the night of the fire, smiled up at him. "A present for you."

Caroline Cotter, her nanny, also smiled,

but hers was more subdued. She blushed. Just as she had that first day when they had boarded the *Hope*. But Mrs Collins was not here to forbid it. The Collins's had paid Caroline's passage in return for her services as a nanny. She was older than Matthew, tall and angular. Her brown eyes were honest and friendly. Often, Caroline had all five of the Collins children with her and it was difficult to talk to her. But today, she only had Alice. Matthew straightened his back, trying to look taller.

Awkwardly, Matthew took the pink ribbon. "I c...can't take this. It's yours."

Alice nodded vigorously, her beaming face upturned as she looked into Matthew's eyes. "Yours."

Caroline shrugged. "You'll never win an argument with a three-year-old. Alice says she wants to thank you."

"There's n...no need. She's thanked me every day for the last w...week."

"You protected her. She might only be three, but she knows that."

Matthew patted Alice's head. "It's b...beautiful. Thanks."

"You're beautiful," she said.

Matthew laughed. "A b...boy can't be beautiful."

"You're beautiful." Alice's voice was louder, more insistent.

She stared up at him as though he was some kind of hero.

"Caroline!"

Caroline jumped nervously at the sound of Mr Collins' voice.

Matthew hoped Caroline would not be scolded for speaking to him. The Collins family demanded every second of her time. But Mrs Collins was even worse than her husband. Her voice was often sharp and petulant. Perhaps she was not feeling well. Her rotund stomach showed she would add another little Collins before the journey was over.

Mr Collins hurried closer. A small, neat man, he always wore a jacket with all the buttons done up. Every morning, a hand mirror in his grasp, he trimmed his moustache with a tiny pair of scissors. Today, he had his jacket done up on the wrong buttons. His hair stuck up in an unruly manner, his face was strangely pale.

"Caroline, leave little Alice with me. Mrs Collins needs you at once!" Mr Collins ran a hand through his hair.

Matthew felt a surge of anxiety. Something was dreadfully wrong.

The measles had spread quickly among the passengers. Matthew remembered when he was younger, being ill for days with the measles. A fever made him see odd and impossible things. His thirst had not been quenched no matter how much water he had drunk. But he had been one of the lucky ones. Six children and two adults from his street had died.

Caroline had not ventured above decks for days. Her hours were spent nursing the sick Collins children and propping up Mrs Collins, who threatened to collapse with anxiety and the effects of her condition. As soon as he had eaten, he would visit the Collins family to see how they were faring.

The ship leaned to the right. Matthew tightened his grip on his bowl of boiled, salted beef and cabbage.

"Don't come back for more," Cook reminded them every day, usually while waving a cooking instrument above his head. "This is your lot and too bad."

Matthew did not like the cabbage and vinegar. It tasted awful and made his stomach gurgle. The first day cook had served it up to them, Timothy had seen Matthew sniff at the cabbage. "If you have half a brain in your head, lad, you'll be eating all of it," he had advised him. "Then you won't be getting the scurvy. I've seen men's legs eaten by so many ulcers they looked like something the rats had been at."

He did not want holes in his legs, and he wanted to please Timothy. So he had eaten it every time it was served. Besides, today he was ravenous.

A cockroach scuttled across his feet. He halted, let it run past, then continued. They weren't much bother. But he did have to remember to shake out his shoes in the morning before sliding them onto his feet.

The *Hope* tilted a little further.

"It's getting rough," said Roger, from behind him.

Matthew had no need to turn around. He knew that Roger would have his friend, Pete, in tow and his eyes trained on Matthew's back. The sea wasn't rough. What was Roger talking about? It was a little choppy, that was all. Roger had a knack for appearing when Timothy was elsewhere. Did he plan it that way?

Before Matthew could form another thought, a blow to his back sent him sprawling. Cabbage was splattered on the deck and a lump of meat protruded from a pair of boots beside him.

"Oh no. Look what's happened," said Roger. "Pete, you should learn to balance yourself with the movement of the ship."

Pete's mouth opened and closed twice before he said anything, "But you p..."

"Are you all right?" Roger cut over the top of Pete.

It was obvious that Pete had been about to say that Roger pushed him. Matthew knew it. But he could not prove it.

"It was all so sudden. What a shame." Roger lifted his foot from the salted beef. It looked filthy and unappetising.

Matthew's stomach burned. He wanted to punch Roger, make him sorry.

"You must be starving," said Roger without offering to share his own meal. "Better clean up, Matthew. Someone might skid on that. Could cause a nasty accident. The captain likes a tidy ship."

Roger and Pete left without another word. But Matthew knew they were thinking plenty. And so was he. Matthew scooped up the cabbage and plopped it into his bowl. Matthew wanted to tell Roger what he thought of him. But his words would only tangle themselves in his tongue and Roger would hurt him even more.

Half-sitting, half-lying, Matthew could not get comfortable. A relay of coughs filtered along the bunks. Many of the children were sick now. Three had died.

He gave Alice's fingers a gentle squeeze. Her damp hair stuck to the pillow like wilted weeds. It was warm and steamy now they were in the tropics. All the hatch covers had been removed but, it only made a slight improvement.

He would have liked to roll up his shirt sleeves, but Alice would not let go of his hand. Whenever he tried to ease his fingers free, she stirred, grizzled and pleaded.

He wanted to help her, but could not think of what to do apart from keeping her company. If only his father was here. He had never been short of an idea or two.

"Eyes hurt." Flushed and gleaming with sweat, Alice turned her face to the shadows.

"Keep them shut."

Her grip tightened.

"I w...won't go anywhere," Matthew

reassured Alice. "I'll stay with you for as long as you like."

A loud scream rent the air. Matthew winced. Alice's eyes shot open. Had she recognised her mother's voice? He patted her hand and made reassuring noises. Soon her eyelids flickered and lowered. He did not know how to explain to a three-year-old that her mother was in labour.

Matthew rinsed a cloth in the basin of sea water and placed it on Alice's forehead. It might help bring down her temperature, the ship's surgeon had said. At any rate, it seemed to make her more comfortable.

Fresh water would have been nicer than salt, but it could not be spared. And after weeks at sea, even that was no longer fresh. The smell was so bad it was only drinkable if a small amount of vinegar was added.

"Read me a story," whispered Alice. Her lips moved, but her eyes remained closed.

"I can't r...read," said Matthew, again wishing he could. "And I d...don't have a book."

"Caroline can read." Alice coughed.

"Caroline is helping your m...mother." When the birth pains first began, Caroline looked more frightened than Mrs Collins. At least Mrs Collins had been through this five times before. Matthew had seen horses born, but he was steering clear of Mrs Collins. Women were another matter.

"I c...can tell you a story," said Matthew. "Timothy told me a good one. And it's true." He repeated the story about the Fijian man who felt the wind on his ears, but he added some details of his own.

"Did he have big ears?" whispered Alice, listening intently.

Matthew smiled. "Maybe. But they were good ears."

A hand rested lightly on his shoulder and he turned. "How are you doing, Matthew lad?" Timothy's green eyes were swamped with concern. "Is there anything I could be doing here?"

Matthew looked down at the empty water container. "W...water?"

Timothy bent and scooped up the container with his one hand.

Matthew's gaze slipped past Timothy to the woman who stood directly behind him. The widow, Mrs Gamble. Her smile was as broad as her hairstyle. Streaks of grey hair framed her face while the rest was a frizzy chestnut brown. Shadows cast by the lamp made her eyes look huge and black. These days, Mrs Gamble could always be found near Timothy. She cut his hair, mended his socks and leant on his shoulder when the sea was rough.

Heavy boots clomped on the ladder as a man climbed down in a hurry. He halted before he reached the bottom. "All men on deck. Look lively."

Matthew looked at Timothy. What was going on?

"There's a ship on the horizon, and no flag visible."

Timothy tensed. A word slipped from his lips that, despite the heat, made a chill run down Matthew's spine. "Pirates."

Matthew strained to see more clearly. There was a slight haze in the air.

"It's there all the time in the tropics," Timothy said.

The sails in the distance gradually grew larger as the ship moved towards the *Hope*.

Pirates, the very word made Matthew's heart beat faster. He turned his head and peered up at the quarterdeck. Was Captain Baldwin worried? It was hard to tell. He had a face that was always set like granite.

Whispers ruffled the air. "How many guns do you think they have? Will it come to hand-to-hand fighting? I didn't come all this way to be killed." On and on, it went. On the other hand, some men, like Timothy, simply stood silent and alert.

Matthew shifted his grip on the lump of wood in his hands. It was not much protection against attacking pirates, but it was better than nothing. There were not enough guns to go round. The men had snatched up anything that might strike a heavy blow.

A loud laugh made all heads snap to the left. Roger was clowning around, pretending to shoot a pirate. His face was alight with eagerness. Matthew wondered if Roger's face was the only part of his head that was alive. There didn't seem to be much between his ears.

"It's a brig," said Timothy. "You can see the masts and sails clearly now."

"Do you really think there are p...pirates on board?" asked Matthew.

Timothy shrugged. "Best not take any chances. A pirate knows he'll be hanged if he's caught. He has nothing to lose."

Matthew squeezed the lump of wood, anticipating the moment that someone would try to wrench it from his hands.

An albatross slowly flew past. Matthew felt a chill as he remembered what the sailor, Harry, had told him. "Timothy, is it t...true that an albatross will take the eyes of a man struggling in the sea?"

"There's some that say so."

Hoping it was not true, Matthew looked at the other ship. It was close enough to see the tiny portholes along its side and the ragged sails. It was damaged, perhaps by a storm like the one the *Hope* had battled.

"There's the remains of a flag wrapped around the pole," shouted Timothy. "That's why we couldn't see it. It's one of ours."

"So, they're not p...pirates then." Matthew felt giddy with relief.

"I wouldn't be putting down your weapon just yet. It could be a trap."

Chapter Four

Alice Constance Collins

DAMAGED BY a severe tropical storm and the crew ravaged by illness, the *Daphne* was a sorry sight at close range. As soon as Captain Baldwin was confident the other ship was not hiding pirates, mayhem broke out. When the men thought the other vessel held enemies, they were stern and tense. Now they ran around helter-skelter.

"They all want to write letters back home and pass them to the *Daphne*," said Timothy. "Captain Baldwin will let us pass the letters over, but no-one will board her because of the fever."

Matthew said nothing. He could not write and there was no-one to send a message to, anyway. It was a sore reminder that he was alone. Although, since he had met Timothy, things did not seem so bleak.

"Not all of these p...people can write."

Timothy shook his head. "Excitement is catching."

For some, thought Matthew.

"I never learnt to do writing." Timothy turned to Matthew and grinned. "Mind you, I can do a very handsome X mark."

Matthew grinned back.

"Matthew."

At the sound of his name, he turned to face Caroline. Dark rings circled her eyes and her lips drooped as though they were too tired to be lifted into a smile. Her hair was untidy and her pupils huge. Her lips twitched, but it could not have been called a smile. The strange expression in her eyes sent a shiver down his back.

"Mrs Collins has..." Caroline's voice trailed off.

"Could I be getting you a drink of water now, Miss?" asked Timothy.

She shook her head but licked her lips as if the mention of water had reminded her that she was thirsty.

Matthew waited for her to continue. Had things gone wrong with the birth?

"Mrs Collins has... it's a boy."

"Oh, good." Matthew felt his forehead scrunch into a frown. "It is good, isn't it?"

Caroline nodded. But she did not look happy. Her eyes were suspiciously bright and her usually rosy cheeks were as pale as milk. Her lips moved but no sound came out.

"How's Alice?" he asked, suddenly afraid.

"Not... not good."

"I'll go straight down." He took only two steps before Caroline grabbed his arm in a surprisingly strong grip. Startled, his eyes met hers and, without her saying another word, he knew.

Two hours later, Matthew stood by the gangway, staring down at his boots. Timothy and Mrs Gamble were on his right and Caroline was on his left.

In some strange way, Matthew felt as if they were standing guard. Over him or Alice, he was not sure. Perhaps it was both.

Mr Collins was there, and some of the other passengers, a dozen people in all.

The sun sank closer to the horizon, its red reflection seeping out across the sky and sea. Another time, he would have stopped to admire its fiery beauty. This afternoon, it made little impression on him.

As the captain strode towards them, a small black book in his large hands, the ship's bell sounded. From now on, Matthew decided, he would always hate the striking of a ship's bell.

He felt anger flare inside him. It was not fair. She was only three. He slid his fingers into his pocket and touched the pink ribbon she had given him.

Captain Baldwin began speaking. His voice was deep and measured, his words carefully chosen. Yet it was hard to concentrate, to take in the meaning.

Matthew's eyes slid sideways to the small piece of canvas in which Alice's body was wrapped. It was weighted with two rounds of shot secured at her feet. She looked smaller lying still.

Mr Collins lifted the board on which Alice's shrouded body lay. He rested it on the rail of the gangway.

Caroline gave a little cry. Without thinking, Matthew slipped his hand into hers. She did not snatch back her hand as he half-expected, but gripped his tightly in return.

Captain Baldwin opened the little black book and began to read. The words flowed like a lullaby. Alice's whispered request came back to Matthew, "Read me a story."

Finally, Captain Baldwin nodded to Mr Collins. "Alice Constance Collins, we commit your body to the deep."

There was a slight pause, as though Mr Collins could not let his daughter go, then her canvas-covered body slipped into the water with a splash.

Matthew turned and peered over the side of the ship. The water was so clear and calm, he could see her sinking. He watched her going down, down through the water until she disappeared.

Although it was late and dark, it was just as hot as it had been during the day. What little breeze there had been was now only a puff that hardly moved the sails.

Matthew thought of his father, then of Alice with her toothy grin. Two people he had cared about, and they were both gone.

Matthew stood on the main deck. It was cooler up here than below decks. A flicker of guilt made him feel that it was wrong to be concerned about being comfortable. At least he was alive.

Timothy was awake, too. "I always miss the Northern Star when I sail this far south."

Matthew stared up at the sky. The stars gleamed as though they had been polished.

"But in the south, there's the Southern Cross. A beauty if I ever saw one. You can use it as a compass if you're lost," said Timothy. "I reckon there's more stars here. Course I haven't counted them. Not yet."

"You can't count the stars. There's too many."

"It's fun trying. And it helps me sleep. I never finish the job. Before I know it, I'm catching forty winks and when I wake up, those sneaky stars have gone into hiding."

Timothy was silent for a while, then he added, "You did fine today, Matthew lad. You handled yourself well. Your father would be proud of you."

A lump formed in Matthew's throat. He wanted his father to be proud of him, and he wanted Timothy to think well of him. But he did not feel as though he had earned praise.

"I w...was angry," he said, honestly.

"Aye, and you'd a right to be. A young child went to her last account before she should. But did you take out that anger on someone else?"

"N...no."

"Were you thinking only of yourself?"

"N...not really." He remembered the way Caroline had held onto his hand, even after Alice's body had slipped into the sea.

"A person can't help how they feel, but they can surely help how they act. And you acted just fine."

"Why can't things stay the same?" Matthew burst out.

"I've asked myself that once or twice." Timothy sniffed. "But I'm thinking if water doesn't move, it goes bad. Stagnant. Maybe we would too. And at what point would you be saying stop? Tomorrow might be the best day of your life. And you won't know until you get there."

"Three is not very old."

"Aye, but I'd say she packed a lot into those three years. I've seen ancient ten-year-olds and I once saw a seventy-year-old who had a light in his eyes that nothing could extinguish. If you ignored his weathered skin, you'd have sworn you were looking into the face of a child."

Matthew remembered Timothy's earlier words about not looking back. "D...do you think looking back makes you old?"

"Nothing wrong with thinking about what's past, but you can't live there. It's the looking forward that keeps you going. There was a time when I thought my days were numbered. But here I am."

"How did you get to be so smart?" asked Matthew.

"By doing lots of stupid things and then wondering where I went wrong." Timothy chuckled. "And speaking of stupid things, there's a moon coming up faster than you can say Timothy Maslin. If you sleep with moonlight on your face, it'll go crooked."

Matthew pressed his lips together to stop himself from smiling. How could his friend be so wise one minute and so superstitious the next?

"I'll be along soon," said Timothy.

Silently, Matthew climbed down the ladder to the lower decks. The lamps were out, but he knew the layout of the ship so well now, he did not need one.

He felt his way across to his hammock. His fingers touched the ropes that secured it to the wall pegs. Unlike the first few times trying to climb into the hammock, when he had landed awkwardly on the floor, this time he leapt up and into it in one go. At the same moment his body hit the canvas, his mouth opened in a yelp.

"Keep it down. We're trying to sleep," a voice growled from the darkness.

Muffled sniggers followed. Without being told, Matthew knew who had filled his hammock with cold water. Even on this day, Roger could not leave him alone.

CHAPTER FIVE

A Rescue

SHELTERED FROM the worst of the biting wind, Matthew leant back against the bulwark and thought wistfully of the warmth of the tropics. Each day the wind seemed a few degrees colder, and the skies had turned to grey. He wrapped his fingers around his pannikin of tea and molasses.

Most of the women and children had gone below decks in the last half-hour. One of the men sat on a pile of rope and played a tune on a tin whistle. Automatically, Matthew felt his toes tapping in time.

Mrs Gamble looked up from her book. She wore a small pair of glasses which had slipped down her nose. "Well, it's getting a little cold for me. I might go below."

Matthew wondered what she was reading about, but did not like to ask.

Timothy stood up. "I'll see you down."

"What about you, Matthew?" Mrs Gamble smiled as she pushed her glasses back to their proper position.

Matthew scanned the deck. Roger stood on the other side of the ship. If he knew Matthew was there, he didn't seem to care. He had not looked around once.

"I'll s...stay up here as long as I can. I like the fresh air."

Agnes Gamble laughed and hugged her shawl tightly around herself. "Fresh is one word for it. I'd call it freezing."

Matthew put down his pannikin and stood up, too.

"I'll be back soon, lad," said Timothy. "A bracing wind does a man good."

Mrs Gamble rolled her eyes.

They headed for the hatchway, looking contented, like two pieces of a puzzle that fitted naturally together. It was good to see Timothy looking so happy.

Wind flapped the sails against the mast. A young sailor with an almost bald head scurried past. His hair was growing back and the red scratch marks from the rough shaving had faded. Matthew watched him climb the rigging, glad the crew had only tormented each other and not the passengers when they had crossed the Equator.

The whistle player gave up, gesturing to Matthew that his fingers were too cold to continue.

Matthew looked up. With a rope slung over his shoulder and an iron hook tucked into his belt, the shaved sailor was climbing the rigging. The wind howled through it. It would be awful climbing up there, thought Matthew. He did not want to dwell on how it felt to reach the top and look down. How small would people look from up there?

The *Hope* leaned to the left. In the last few minutes, the wind had increased. The young sailor kept his grip. Did he feel dizzy? Matthew was so engrossed in watching the sailor make his way higher up the rigging, that he flinched when a voice spoke nearby. It was Roger. Matthew missed what he had said, but he would bet it was nothing kind. Roger wore a permanent smirk on his face like a disfigurement.

Suddenly, Matthew sensed movement from above. Something dark and heavy hit the side of Roger's head and bounced to the deck. Roger crumpled sideways. The upper part of his body folded over the bulwark like the plank of a seesaw. Silently, almost gracefully, he pitched over the side of the ship into the heaving sea.

Dumbfounded, Matthew looked down at the deck and saw the metal hook that had been in the young sailor's belt. He looked up again. The young sailor did not seem to have noticed what had happened. No other passengers remained on deck. And the rest of the crew had their hands full struggling with ropes and sails. No-one paid him the slightest attention.

He took two steps to the bulwark and peered over. Already, in those few seconds, the ship was leaving Roger behind. He did not struggle or call out. He simply floated, face down, arms outspread. The hook had knocked him unconscious. Roger would certainly drown.

Matthew ran along the deck, leaping over ropes and dodging obstacles. As he ran, thoughts galloped through his mind. If Roger was to drown, his cruelty would drown with him. Matthew wondered what would happen if he waited a few seconds before calling for help?

Even as the idea formed, he dismissed it. He screamed, "M...man overb...board! Help! Someone help me!"

Frantically, he looked around. A life buoy! He grabbed it from its hook and held back his right arm, ready to hurl it overboard. But how could Roger grab it? He was unconscious. Someone had to help him. No-one would expect Matthew to leap overboard and save him. But it didn't seem right to pick and choose whom you would rescue. If someone was in trouble, you did your best.

Matthew slipped the buoy over one arm and heaved himself up. Balanced with one leg over each side of the bulwark, he took a deep breath and threw himself into the sea.

As his body hit the water, it closed over his head. Paralysed with cold and shock, he did not move at first. Then he bobbed to the surface and took a huge breath. He hung onto the life buoy, looking left and right. A wave lifted him up.

There! A patch of brown riding the waves, some distance away. Kicking as hard as he could and hanging onto the buoy with fearsome grip, Matthew headed toward Roger.

Each time he thought he was getting closer, a wave would knock him further back. Matthew clenched his jaw and kicked harder. Grey, everything was grey. There was nothing beyond this grey coldness.

Please don't let there be anything hungry swimming underneath me, thought Matthew. He had seen several sharks and one whale on this journey. And he had no wish to see them at closer range.

Breathing heavily, his lungs on fire and his legs screaming at him to stop, he reached Roger. He stretched out his right arm to grab Roger but a surge of curling white water pushed him away.

A few strong kicks brought him back again. This time he grabbed Roger's hair and lifted his face clear of the water.

Matthew felt exhausted. His mouth tasted like salt and his eyes stung. He could not hold Roger like this for long.

Timothy wrapped a blanket around Matthew's body. "It's all right, lad. You're safe now." Matthew's teeth chattered so much it made his head ache. His arms, legs, lungs were all protesting. He tried to speak, but his lips were numb with cold.

"Don't you try to speak," said Timothy. "You must be stronger than you look. That was some feat hanging onto a man that size while we got a boat back out to you."

Matthew chewed his bottom lip, "R...Roger?"

Roger lay prone on the deck, his head to one side. His eyes were closed and his face, white as chalk.

Timothy squeezed Matthew's arm. "I'm telling you, my heart almost jumped out of my chest when I saw you leap over the side. I'm too old for such frights, lad. Don't you be fretting about that young man now. You did your best. And you should see yourself. You look worse than he does."

"H...he's dead, isn't he?" Matthew struggled to sit.

The ship's surgeon ineffectually tapped and prodded Roger's unconscious form. He seemed to be making no progress.

Timothy clicked his tongue impatiently. "Out of the way, man." He stormed over to where Roger lay.

The surgeon blustered. "What do you think you're doing?"

Timothy pushed him aside. "I've seen more half-drowned men than you've had hot dinners. No offence, now."

Vigorously, he began pushing on Roger's back as though he was trying to force him into the lower deck. Push, push.

"I will protest to the captain," shouted the surgeon. "You'll kill this man."

"The sea might do that yet. But not if I can help it. Now pipe down, will you kindly? You'll be giving me the earache."

Suddenly a burst of seawater erupted from Roger's mouth. It looked like the spout of a whale.

Timothy pushed again at Roger's back and a second spurt of water shot over the deck. Then Roger began to cough. Timothy sat back on his heels.

Roger coughed hard and long. Then he rolled onto his side. Loud coughing gripped him again and he spat water onto the deck. It even ran from his nostrils. Then, he caught Matthew's eyes and his lips pressed together in a hard line. "What are you looking at, runt?"

Chapter Six

A Promise Kept

CAROLINE BLUSHED when she caught Matthew's eye. She quickly returned to scouring the horizon. The gale had blown itself out and the weather was again moderate. But there was enough wind to make good speed.

"Are you sure we'll see land soon?" she asked Timothy.

"Aye."

Roger sauntered past, sneering. In the weeks since Matthew had saved him, there had not been one kind word from him. No questions, no suggestion of gratitude.

Strangely, Matthew did not care. He felt hot pins and needles at the memory of how close he had been to letting Roger die. How could he have considered that, even for a second? It was not his right to say whether someone should live or die.

What had Timothy told him the night they watched the stars? You can't help how you feel, but you can help how you act.

Caroline's voice carried a shrill note of excitement. "What's that?"

"It's a wave, dear," said Mrs Gamble.

"Oh." Undaunted, Caroline still stood on her toes, straining to see.

Matthew's emotions tumbled inside him. He longed for this journey to end, but he hated the thought of parting from Timothy.

As if he shared his thought, Timothy cleared his throat. "I'm thinking that when we reach Australia, we'll most likely be needing a strong pair of hands to help us."

Matthew did not look at Mrs Gamble, but he did not miss Timothy's use of the word "we". He knew what it meant. It was good that Timothy would not be alone.

"I've got some money put aside and I'm aiming to breed sheep. I have a feeling the future's in sheep. Would you be kind enough to consider a job with us when we land, Matthew lad? Not much money and lots of hard work, that's all we can offer you."

Matthew pressed his lips together so they would not tremble. "I'd like that."

Timothy sighed, as though he had been afraid Matthew would refuse.

Mrs Gamble nodded, "It wouldn't be the same without you."

"I'm going to find a handsome husband and live in a nice house," said Caroline.

Mrs Gamble laughed. "I shall learn to like sheep."

"What about you, Matthew lad?" asked Timothy.

"I'm g...going to learn to read." Matthew fingered the pink ribbon he kept in his pocket.

Caroline screamed, her finger stabbing the air. "I can see it. The new land."

Matthew squinted against the glare. Yes, there it was. A shadow on the edge of the sea.

"Land-ho," called a sailor from the crow's nest above them.

A thrill of excitement shook Matthew. It was real. He had travelled halfway round the world. He had kept his promise to his father, and now he was looking at his future.